Book of Spells

Book of Spells

poems

Gary Lemons

Red Hen Press | *Pasadena, CA*

Book layout by Mark E. Cull
Interior illustrations by Heidi Stiles

Library of Congress Cataloging-in-Publication Data

Names: Lemons, Gary, author.
Title: Book of spells : poems / Gary Lemons.
Description: First edition. | Pasadena, CA : Red Hen Press, 2025.
Identifiers: LCCN 2024018666 (print) | LCCN 2024018667 (ebook) | ISBN 9781636281940 (trade paperback) | ISBN 9781636282503 (hardcover) | ISBN 9781636281957 (ebook)
Subjects: LCGFT: Poetry.
Classification: LCC PS3612.E475 B66 2025 (print) | LCC PS3612.E475 (ebook) | DDC 811/.6—dc23/eng/20240429
LC record available at https://lccn.loc.gov/2024018666
LC ebook record available at https://lccn.loc.gov/2024018667

The National Endowment for the Arts, the Los Angeles County Arts Commission, the Ahmanson Foundation, the Dwight Stuart Youth Fund, the Max Factor Family Foundation, the Pasadena Tournament of Roses Foundation, the Pasadena Arts & Culture Commission and the City of Pasadena Cultural Affairs Division, the City of Los Angeles Department of Cultural Affairs, the Audrey & Sydney Irmas Charitable Foundation, the Meta & George Rosenberg Foundation, the Albert and Elaine Borchard Foundation, the Adams Family Foundation, Amazon Literary Partnership, the Sam Francis Foundation, and the Mara W. Breech Foundation partially support Red Hen Press.

First Edition
Published by Red Hen Press
www.redhen.org

for Nöle-ji—

the wand bearer

Contents

I have gone out, a possessed witch,
haunting the black air, braver at night;
dreaming evil, I have done my hitch
over the plain houses, light by light:
lonely thing, twelve-fingered, out of mind.
A woman like that is not a woman, quite.
I have been her kind.

—Anne Sexton

. . . There where the vines cling crimson on the wall,
And in the twilight wait for what will come.
The leaves will whisper there of her, and some,
Like flying words, will strike you as they fall;
But go, and if you listen she will call . . .

—Edward Arlington Robinson

What cannot be said will be wept.

—Sappho

Preface

Language changes. It molds itself to while offering a door out of the time in which it's understood. When it doesn't change—when it stagnates—the diseases of mind and body proliferate. Racism—misogyny—homophobia—the well-known cruelties of this and likely every epoch crystallize into qualities children inherit and without learning a new language it becomes nearly impossible to resist prejudices and dissemble weapons affixed in the cradle.

Language casts ripples—spells if you will—each thought alters the flight of birds—every word distributes profound sensation—each falling leaf changes the world—gather these up—the real magic of wind—of fire—of children—of love—they will provoke new words that come out of silence—into paintings—dances—relationships—poems.

We live and breathe and move through a topology of magic—this is the ambedo—the hypnotic attention to everything in detail all at once that builds an invisible bridge between intuition and action—the creative *force hypermechanique* between all things—the magic of aliveness.

Yet we live from the cave to present moment in a near constant state of war. With ourselves and others. Individual peace is difficult to find and harder to maintain. National peace is fleeting and fragile—we are made of the same recycled material yet still devolve generation to generation with more weapons than tools to create an inhabitable grace.

The poems in here are likely one poem which is why—with the exception of Cloud Spell and Mountain Spell and Liquid Spell—they are all called Spell. The division between pages and starred stanzas is entropic—order at best is a temporary imposition—and within any single poem the starred sections can be read without reference to what came before or after—no past—no present.

So here we are now—it is easy to believe we are alone—big countries still eat up small countries—weapons are brandished to scare already frightened animals into making immoral choices—the shrinking resources of the planet are distributed into fewer hands—everyone is or will soon be a soldier often for a cause they don't believe in.

It falls to the artists and scientists—mothers and fathers—the children—as it has throughout time to replace the old commandments chiseled on stone tablets and followed for millennia. Time for magic—for a new vocabulary that allows this—it's time—as Rilke said so beautifully—to become the living answers to the questions few are willing to ask.

Cloud Spell

None of this is real
And all of this is real—

What if this is the last time your
Dog lies in the sunlight
At your feet or your cat purrs
In your lap while you read
Love letters from a friend.

What if this is the last time
You hear Andrea Bocelli sing
From his darkness to yours
About the light between you.

What if this is the last time
You walk in the cold rain
Shivering inside a jacket too
Thin for the season.

What if this is the last
Time you recognize your name.

What if this is the last time
An internal jury imposes
A life sentence on your soul.

What if this is the last time
You gasp with the little pleasure

Of a touch or look through both sides
Of a window that won't open.

What if this is the last time
You wake up strewn with flowers
In a dump truck on the way to heaven.

What if the flowers say
Your name just as you
Escape their obsession with light
But you don't know who you are
Unless they bloom in you.

What if this is the last time
You're damaged by church
Bells or barbells.

What if for the last time the stain
Glass windows above the altar
Show dark angels eating biscuits
And gravy without handcuffs and little
Cherubs throwing halos in the soup
Served behind the barn
To those hungering for grace
On the installment plan.

What if this is the last time
You're alive and the dead are dead
And the distinction is important.

What if there's no whiskey drool
On the pillow shared with a ghost.

What if the total of your comforts
Subtracted from your discomforts equals zero.
Or plus or minus one.

What if a hand comes out of a hole
And slaps you awake and you are
The light trapped inside bacon.

What if you could be what you dreamed
Before they bottled your youth
To resuscitate antiquarian glands.

What if you caused no one pain—caused
No one sorrow—held no one back—kept

No secrets—told no lies and still
Came home to an empty house.

What if you gave everything
Away because owning anything is
To drown in the kiddie pool.

What if this is the last time
Your hair falls out and your blood
Pressure rises and your cough worsens

And the song in your throat surges
Through the heartwood to become the syrup
Used to sweeten the buns of a queen.

What if everything is exactly perfect
And all imperfection is a jacket
Worn by Jesus or Houdini.

What if someone loves you
And you know this even when depressed—
Even when the metallurgists pound
You into a blade—even as the shovel
Lifts a past life from the ground.

What if for the last time
The darkness folds you on a shelf
Where you lie clean and fresh
Wanting to be worn.

What if for the last time
You see your mother in the face
Of the storm as it deposits
Lipstick on your upturned cheek.

What if for the last time
You slept in a red thimble of rain
And exhales pollen.

Who are you—

Stagger into it—dance
Alone or accompanied—into it—drunk
On options and choices—or accidents—
Follow the optics into the next into
The next toward the flickering candle
In the broken window

Of a house that isn't there
Until you build it.

Spell

Spell

At dawn I met the men
On street corners central
To our neighborhood—the twinkle
Of cigars is the first light I see
As the dawn whispers far away—
The hot ash falls on my hair
When they lean over to make sure
I pack the bundles right—

We're always delivering something—
Sometime for money—sometime
Because no one else will—today I take my feet
Out of my shoes and tip toe into
My wife's room to replace the oxygen tank
And adjust her pillows while
She dreams—I hope—of beautiful
Dresses swaying at the hem around her
Young legs when we danced forty years

Ago beneath a moon so bright
It blinded us to the days to come.

Spell

A child stands in wonder
At a thing she thought lived
Only in stories—she sees
Slow lightening inside a glass bowl
Where soft little turtles brought
Home in plastic bags explore
Transparent prison walls.

The half-life of childhood is less than
The blink of a turtle's eye—old
And wise in the egg—born knowing the
Inexhaustible spirit—expecting no
Quarter from touch or wave—rocked
By the salt in its blood that's
What's left of its home—

The turtles tremble as the toilet
Flushes them back through rivers
To the sea—like leaves from a burning tree
Floating through space to set another tree
On fire—they will not be silenced—

Or Paul—on the road to Damascus—
Cursing and swatting at angels
While becoming one.

Spell

The door slams in the house
Falling to ruin beneath birch trees
Where the poetry of life bubbles up
From limestone caves through dogwood
Flowers to heckle trout in yellow
Creeks turned red by rotting logs.

A fist falls on the family Bible—
Becomes a bird slamming into a window—
Somewhere in those terrible fables
The road to Jericho cracked open from wagons
Wheeling bottles of doom to those who
Judge everyone but themselves.

At any moment a sharpened
Stick in the form of prayer may
Push through the brain and out the sneer
To stab anyone brave enough
To row a cadaver out to the vanishing
Point of this red silence.

We never know—until we know—
How much we can bear—or which
Burdens turn into blessings
When we set them down.

Spell

A skinny child—boy
Or girl—don't matter—
Staring at a line of friends with
Their hands joined—
A hard line—hands
Gripped tight—gonna keep
You out—a wall which only
The determined or crazy might break
With luck and courage—
And of course the heart thumping
Fear of being left out.

Red Rover Red Rover
Send someone right over—

I charged the line—hit the
Weakest link with all my strength—
Two girls—maybe 10 years old—way smaller
Than me with braces and zits
And bangs in knee length
Skirts with tennis shoes
And ankle socks—hit the place

Where their hands gripped one
Another—hit them at a full run—
But I couldn't break them—

Their hands held—I bounced
Back unable to enter—small—raggedy—
A power in them like whispers
In old telephone wires—they
Held—they were sisters—

They held.

Spell

The bare wire between lovers amplifies touch.—
Sends shockwaves through generations—
Morning glories on the fallen shed—unbelievers
Awake in the front row pew—

The redwood slowly spins
As a couple hugs it—the sky
Blushes—do we touch one another
And for how long—questions marigolds solve by blooming—
Leaving us breathless in the national
Park we've made of offices.

So bring everything you own
As an offering to the wilderness described
So vividly in the book no one's written
Because no one returned—bring
Parachutes and the rake Auden took
From the gardener—bring dried flowers—
Their blood still wet from childhood—bring
Tears cried for the self—bring

Everything you own—bring everything
I should say—you borrowed.

Spell

The prisoner is guilty of heresy.
She mocked the beards of the patriarchs.
She placed asterisks on the powerful.

She stood beside the children.
She fed the homeless with pieces
Off her perfect body.

She murdered decorum
And dressed in the uniform of flowers
Then shared fluids with stones.

She calls the fallen angels
By name—one at a time—
Dragonfly—elephant—polar bear—bee.

She locked down on soldiers
With silent trumpets in her smile.

She stepped on the toes
Of founding documents whose promises
Are the only known lubricant
To restore a father's gun.

The prisoner is asked
By inquisitors what she'd
Like to eat before wheeled
Into the room where nothing

Matters to the acolytes of Torquemada
Except the expressions
On the doctor's face as he taps
Deeply into the bluest vein—the blue
Of wax candles simmering
Above hatchling swans—injecting
In succession three poisons
That tumble toward the heart like kayakers
Descending waterfalls—into the body
Of the prisoner in a ritual

As old as any corn god
Astride a virgin with his knife.

She rejects the fried chicken.
She rejects the barbecued ribs
And the ice cream and pie.

Asks—for her last supper—

Earth in the mouth to taste the
Iron of birth—the sediment
Of sisters as they mineralize—
Give her feathers found
On mountaintops—she'll eat
Current from swift rivers—she'll
Swim among the sparkling reflections
In the lost and found.

The woman is no longer
Imprisoned by the registered gaze—
Her innocence smolders underground
While men in soiled britches dig
Graves for their cigars—

She is free from the bloodless
Friars who smuggle machine guns
Inside a glove—free to question the Magi
Who come under the flag of commerce
Calling brotherhood a gift.

Earth trembles and dreams
In her iron forest—exchanges carbon
With stars as she dreams—liquid trees
Grow from her silence above fires

Where scared children watch
Stooped creatures with bloody
Hands scratch commandments
On tablets made of skin.

Spell

In the air memories waver
Where thought hangs its oxidized bell
Waiting to be rung—to ring out
In praise of sweet necessities—of meadows
Where dragonflies flit above the
Shadows they make in flight—

When the bell is struck
Its voice appears as if by magic—
Though it hangs in front of us the clapper lives
In a different animal than
The one we are now.

What moves the veil to comfort
The darkness on both sides of it—
To conduct the silence in the roots
Into the bower's greenery—to say the thing
Out loud that reveals desire's footsteps
On the path we left behind.

The bell sobs as it rings
But cannot return to the quiet
Grace before it was struck.

None of us can.

Spell

The child put to sleep by sirens—
The adults picking window glass from
Each other's hair—the dog drowning
In a crater of rain—wake up singing
Elegies to no one at all because no one has
Died—the grip holding the door
Closed will let go and strangely enough
The excitement of the grim reaper juggling
Hearts in a minefield will turn to terror
The moment the flowers bloom.

Already there are elderly parents
Locked in overheated rooms trying
To lick the moonlight off a photograph
Of hummingbirds—there are magnetic bees flitting
Through steel canyons looking for pollen
In the fossils of a gun—

We stretch but remain standing—
We reach but never touch—until we
Live into and through one another—mapping with
A shared hand the strategic ground
Everyone must fly over to prove
They have no shadow.

Spell

In a frozen prison library
Sylvia Plath catalogues
Books—chipping them with a hammer
From the ice—placing them on her tongue
To warm the elegant vowels trapped
Inside conformist sentiment.

Beside her Emily Dickinson
Patches the spines of venerable
Tomes with ectoplasm scraped
From the moustache of a ghost
That leans over her shoulder blowing
Voluminous shimmering bubbles
Of beef boiled in aftershave.

A new book ordered centuries
Ago arrives. It has no pages and no title
And is full of no ideas
But is nonetheless burned
By the electorate who object
To their diaries made public.

Elizabeth Bishop watches
This from the top shelf—
She knows the lies from the past
Are sailing ships with broken masts
At the mercy of currents—that

Any fragment of truth is a hungry
Bear dripping dark honey from a rotten
Tree on the beards of blue iris.

And so they catalogue
Yesterday while comforting today—these
Phantom limbs of Eve—independent
Of their bodies—holding out
The apple—saying—here it is—
Take it—then

Tell us not how
It tastes but how heavy it is
In your hand.

Spell

The sun lifts above the rim of
The earth and erases the stars
Like thoughts steal words from
Other thoughts leaving both bereft
Of substance—maybe like the dead they
Wander inside the misperception
They are forgotten.

We awaken early—the cat is disturbed
By whoever threw off the covers
But someone must witness the stars
Swallowed by the morning—Orion—
Antares—Betelgeuse—we hold each one
In sight as long as possible so
When they fade away we might
Still remember them—

Mother—brother—child.

Spell

Across inundated fields
Lightning sets fire to weathervanes
On houses still visible above the rising flood—
Parents hold their children up beneath peaked
Roofs—standing on piled boxes
As the air pocket shrinks—somewhere
Not far away ducks flounder in mud
At the edge of a freeway—

I dance among these tragedies
With you in my arms to the music
Of the life we tried to keep forever—sweat
Running down our legs—the drums
Getting louder as we share mouth
To mouth the sweet pollen
From the devil's garden—all
The while pushing an enormous
Stone uphill that like

The world is too heavy to bear
And not really there.

Spell

* * *

The medic is ancient but hasn't aged.

It carries the wounded on litters
In a thousand wars—never forgets a face
In the library of grief where the rising moon
Stiffens the bindings around sorrow
And the pressure between closed eyes
Exsanguinates to silver the rank confetti
Spraying souls back at the night.

It touches the light—the pulse—
The flood—first with fingertips.

* * *

In the night the medic glides
To the wounded soldier.

She's been hit twice in the vest
That saved her, once in the leg as
Torn arteries seep through
Her uniform into the dirt.

It touches her—morphine, tourniquet,
Wipes her face and then, as she sleeps
Licks a tiny drop of blood—both are saved
By the restraint it takes to blow only once
Into a horn with your last breath.

The medic moves on. It blends.
Corpsmen see it and nod.
There's always the next wounded

Thing—the next and the endless next
War shoveling dirt over a poem.

Sometimes it happens that
The medic is found out. Some suspicious
Movement—seen cherishing
Exposed bone or telltale smears
On the lips of its bistoury—

Blessed the caretakers that take nothing—
Blessed the purple hearts in vineyards by the sea—

Blessed be the protein unbound from desire—
Blessed the ones who walk away
From the wars that never end—

Blessed be the ones who follow.

Spell

Once the artist changed the straw
In the manger—wiped up the spilled oil—
Painted the mules—fumigated the kings
Then changed their diapers.

It then exposed the breasts
Of the women and set the cradle
Out on the curb for tomorrow's pickup
And finally unbound the whole story from
The fustian nonsense that birthed it—

No one looking into this diorama
Felt the need for prostration—rather—
Minds split like old jeans as the imagination
Escaped through the bunghole of belief—leaving
Families working hard to eradicate the virus
Spread by influencers that split theit tongues
To speak in dead languages.

And who fog the windows inside the stores
Where tomorrow is on sale—today
Is sold out and yesterday is free.

Spell

At first I believed everything
I was told—that Jesus loved the little
Children—*red and yellow—black and white—they*
Are precious in his sight—stuff that made me
Proud at 8 to be a Christian.

But children's songs sung by adult
Voices often lose their way and by 10 I knew
No one believed in anything but the faithless
Words of twisted prophecy as removed
From the original meaning as sand
From ground down mountain tops.

So I let go of the rope and fell—
Like all believers—reaching terminal
Velocity at the impact point
With ignorance and presumption then dying
Into disbelief—which I
Learned is just another reliance
That takes more than it gives.

And yet—everyone is out of breath
When they're born.

Spell

The time of innocence
Fades so slowly it sometimes
Never leaves at all—its smoke
Lingers in dreams like wildfire
In the notes of birds.

I thought stink bugs got
Their name because they farted—
I thought dragonflies shot flames at little boys
And bats played baseball between
The stars—really—I believed
Words meant what they said—

Once in the woods my father identified
The sweet song of a titmouse—when I got
Home and no one was looking i went through
My mother's brassieres looking for birds.

I think of this now as she shifts
On her bed—dying while the winter light
Through the blinds leaves stripes
Across her disappearing face.

Then it's over—she's gone.
And in the silence birds begin sing.

Spell

The orchid loves the velvet lips of night—
The cooling respite from the burning sun—
She smears the greasy moon upon her coat—
Is supplicant to the coming undone—
She moans up at the stars like a lover
Turning exhaustedly away in bed—
Her moist petals opening in the dark—
Her candle aloft for the stars to see.

Under these circumstances the roses
Are embarrassed to require so much sun—
How they suffer under Venus and Mars—
Frightened by the dark—beyond the last chance—
Like fish that lose their color on a hook.
All these worshippers of excessive light.

Every moment magnifies the silence—
What good is a prophet that never speaks?

Spell

I grew up without a mother
In a house filled with women.

I ended up in the pink and black
Desoto all of one Saturday so as
We'd be down by the river
For the baptism in which
I was the main event.

About 9 years old standing
In the Shenandoah River shivering
In a white sheet beneath which
My naked body trembled
While the choir clog-danced
On green planks set across hay bales
On the bank and the preacher
Pushed his unshaven face into mine
Saying—now child—

Now—then with a neat trick
I later used on my brother—tripped
Me with his foot and dunked me
Under and held me while I stared
Up at the cottonwoods and the blue
Sky through a cold green current.
When he pulled me back up
I lay my head on his shoulder
And cried while the choir struck

Up The Old Wooden Cross
And he whispered in my ear—
Saved boy—saved—you ain't
Never got to be afraid again.

So yeah—saved—not like
A dollar in the bank or a soul
Released by those who pray for it
But like an old axe in the shed

That's gone through generations
Of wooden handles and waits
Patiently for another one
To be of use again.

Spell

Study the works of wolves—
Bishop—Guthrie—Chief Joseph—
Gale—Schiffmann—Stevens—Sexton—
Giulini—Coltrane—Plath—

Fumble in the perpetual twilight
Of a darkroom shuffling negatives
Of ghosts inside the body that don't
Want to be seen—find the switch but don't turn it on—
Develops the poem in the dark bathed
By solvents in memory's tray—see the past materialize
From faces that can no longer look away.

Through no skill we grow old—
Less enamored with dark rooms
Or prologues to inspire book clubs—we
Water the violets on a windowsill—

Sing to a dying land
From a softening shell—

Hear the tide call for justice
In the sonorous voice of a white
Bear on shrinking ice
Giving vent to its hurt and hunger
In low C below the second E
As it turns in smaller circles

Around a last refuge melted by
Malicious indifferences.

Isn't this enough now?

Spell

My friend's mother was an anarchist
Who loved to throw apples through a tire
Hung from a rope to refine her aim when
The time came to place the Molotov
Cocktail exactly through the open
Window of the limousine.

This precision in preparation
For a horrible end is why
Chess players practice pinching
Small grains of cooked rice together
Before sacrificing a pawn.

Years might go by before
We catch a ride on the tractor coming
Back from the promised land
Covered with incisors from scraping
The horizon off the tongue
Of those who market emptiness.

My grandmother exchanged
Recipes with the anarchist
But never had her to dinner.

Grandmother wasn't always
A Christian though—she shaved her legs
Down by the creek and hid them in men's
Trousers so her parents didn't know—

She kissed boys in the barn with lips
As urgent as swifts in the loft.

She once said—hugging me
Goodnight—say your prayers—do
What you're told unless it's wrong and whenever
The urge comes to throw bombs
At limousines sit down at a desk—

Take out a sheet of paper
And set the damn thing on fire
With words.

Spell

Some things are stranded inside
Water and some things inside fur
And all things inside each other but nothing
Ends up where it started including
This bent stick wandering beneath
A sunset turned pink from the dreams
Sucked out tenement windows.

This is strong medicine to swallow—
Easy to imagine it can awaken
The blind hermit in its drift log
Castle contemplating the question—

Why do fascist urinators gather
Around a burning flag waiting
For orders to put the fire out?

Tomorrow smokes on a frozen
Hill where the flailing of red scarves
Awakens the birds of prey in time
To descend upon the spectators

Who follow their leaders back into the cave
Where they were engineered.

Spell

When interior winds blow down
The baskets of impatiens on the porch—
Then whirl them into place again—
Her hands might turn into paws—
The shoulders grow wings—the feet
Become fins—the weight become
Weightless as she races and flies
And swims through previously closed doors
Like a new kind of woman living
In the pauses between breath.

The dance is not only movement—nor
Necessarily innocent as a pulse in the
Jugular of grace—more a flickering candle
Flame looking out from the wick
At the shadows on the world
Made from its brief light—maybe

Love spilling from a thimble—
Swimming upstream—back
To the source of all tears.

Spell

Growls around fire—
Pluck of strings—rustle
Of nylons in a taxi—long exhalations
Loosed like sprinters near
A finish line—

Songs of praise—promises—oh—
Atonements for the deed—loud loud louder—
Hard winds making the aspens dance—
Remember every leaf shaking
Above the poisoned wolf—

Ribs underfoot in fast food
Joints—bath tub drain clogged
With hair—trillium reaching
For autumn light as nightingales
Push blue notes around a field
In the wheelbarrow of a song—

Let the mind find the heart—
Let the voices whisper to the ghost
Of the melting wolf—let all things alone—

Let the aspens teach us to dance
When there is no wind.

Spell

The silent panther blends into
The winter night unseen in the falling snow
By hunters feeling its body heat
In their trigger fingers—

There's a momentary ripple
In the quantum of slender trees—
Bullets fumbled by cold hands fall
Into the snow that sticks
To the hunters—to even the silence—

There's a great circle everything
Walks on its way home—unbound by
Brief insights or sudden clarity—
Suffering or the confusion of prayers softening
To a curse around a bitten tongue.

One life—two lives—
How many before this awakening
No longer hurts?

Mountain Spell

* * *

As the wind fails the rowers
Sweat beneath the inkling smear
Of night—a rose crushed under
A black slipper—north star just
Visible over the prow—the king
Levers the pendulum beneath his damp
Robe before—after too much that's forbidden—
Pushing his daughter overboard—
Assuring heirs will strike oil here.

We are looking away when
This happens—there is so much else
Than these unpleasantries to behold
With affection—the heat pipes make noise—someone
With a spoon is raising hell in a bowl
While the royal barge rows away
From ripples in the luminous salt
Beneath which daughters sing
In a vortex of bubbles.

* * *

But this is not the story
Of the girl in the Victorian bonnet
With bloody gloves asking
The men with axes to stop
Chopping trees in the prologue—

Too late—everything is happening
Again—this is the smooth symmetry
Gold miners understands—how the bright
Seam becomes a mouth that sputters
Madness at a headlamp—how
Little we see even in the light—how
Our suffering is mixed with desire
Into ingots of false gold.

How the stopping of wind
Dissuades the king from spitting
On the shadows of the cameleers—how
The Bactrian camel—lost in wisdom—
Alone know the 100th name of god—the one
That if spoken unifies all faiths.

✶ ✶ ✶

if anything is true then
Time evaporates grief
Into love and back again—

Days like new foliage
After wildfire—a pastel orchid
Clinging to the burnt tree falling
Into its ashen family—and the purple
Feather stuck to a thorn as green
Fiddleheads uncurl toward the sun
Where the shrike is hiding.

Daylight saturates the black earth
Like birth rags in a bucket—
Hence the landlord at the center
Of war's baroque expectancy milks
The gland swollen with moisture
Derived from a dress—the rent
Overdue—the city abandoned—

The jets overhead dropping
Bleach on the stains.

* * *

There's something so cold
In the fire it is impervious to heat—

The snowflakes melt down
Into the mouth of a soldier
Urinating in her grave—in a clearing
A machine gun lies useless—
This is a retreat and there's
No time to reload—the snake we inherit
Is the grandfather telling
This story while twirling his helmet
With a finger in the bullet hole—

* * *

Someone is always bathing inside
Another—perhaps the sound of water

In the skull reminds you of afternoons
Spooning reflections from a lily pond—

We should never have looked at her—
The edge where she considers falling
Into the life she hates for no reason
Other than she hasn't lived it
But wants to try—to live that is.
No longer only a daughter—
And other expectancies.

✳ ✳ ✳

We should have taken up
Spinning like a barber pole
Not a Sufi fire eater spitting
Carbon sucked from stars—

We should not hate one
Another more than we love
One another—the tea kettle

Boils its song in the air—the goat
In the marketplace—yes—
The one with flies on its nose—

Sings that same song as we sip
Our bitter tea in the shade.

* * *

In an immortal bed of light Ra
Kisses Osiris—the twins exchange
Requests for sublingual afterlives
Involving visitations from wildflowers
Yearning for more battlefields—

But for now—may the flowers—
Assembled in the moonlight—glimpse
Through the broke cypress two
Bodies becoming one candle—twins—
Four hands—four eyes following
The apogee of one moon—one flame—

We live in a room with a door
That never opens—there's tea stains
On the antimacassar but no one wants
Out—we're not alone—the cat walks
Anywhere it wants but won't

Stop licking its tail—the room
Has only one door but no walls—

Perhaps we are alone just not here—
Out there—with no way home.

＊ ＊ ＊

The birth of a god requires
The simultaneity of two believers
Fighting for primacy inside a prophet's words—scuba
Divers with the bends—sharing oxygen
From one tank as they ascend.

If the lights go off inside your diary
Please don't say I didn't warn you—

Bulbs must be changed—we burn out—
In the dark we learn to remember
Our regrets often brush the hair
Of some old truth used to barter affection
For pain—or some other currency
Depleted by inflation—or perhaps the author—
Who insists we believe every story—
Is overcome by a lust for fiction

While drinking from a new idea
In the desert beneath a golden sky where
Blue wolves stand ready to
Swallow the red light of the sun.

＊ ＊ ＊

Deciphering the funerary texts—

Inside the stone vault pollen
From thousand year old flowers

Lies heavy on the palimpsest
Protected by an ivory statue
Of a slender cat—the flowers are also
Lipstick on the rim of an unwashed
Cup—the living dust of time
Glitters in the headlamps—the scarab
Placed here by Mother Time
Was not born to leave—

We seem to mind nothing
These days—take it all in and let it go
Without feeling anything—like
A child halved by a custody suit
Or matadors gored by adoration
Rather than bulls.

* * *

This morning I promise to tell
No lies but simply by writing this
I snap a long icicle off the frozen
Roof and swallow it before it melts—

Sunset arrives like a horseshoe crab
Dunked glowing red from a kettle
Into the aspirations of an unshod horse.

* * *

One hermit is not a story—two
Hermits together are not hermits—
What this means is alone or accompanied
We must determine our own value
Before we're counted or discounted—

What comes next which is why
The pharaohs soaked their calves
In the milk of wolves—doesn't want to
To know the length of its shadow
Striding away—is disembodied like
Fossils inside a rock—comes apart when
The questions hide in big waves
Inundating fields of corn—

This is as it should be—the evolution
Begins in the future whereas
The revolution is over now—
Simon says.

✳ ✳ ✳

The child was just told
To go to bed and his face
Is red but instead of crying
He just hides from himself—

Not for the first time
Do the lilacs rattle the window

Despite no wind—letting
Themselves frolic in premonitions
Knowing summer will end—
They will freeze into a dream
And their roots will sip the blood
Of soldiers—of dinosaurs—any
Rotted thing—while watching
Monarchs suck up communal fires
Then spit out lightning bolts

Meanwhile the twins see the end
Of oneness is the beginning of violet
Circles under the eyes—an orchid feeding
On the characters in a fairy tale—on the chin
Perhaps—rooted in the mouth
That kisses the turnip freshly
Popped from dark soil—every confessional
Is the meadow in which carnivorous
Flowers lie dormant until something
Wet awakens them—rain—tears—
Whatever comes apart when trapped.

* * *

What the bride won't tell you
Is to lay in the lotus flower half
Asleep is to be fully aroused—

Speaking of which an old man
Wakes up in a white sheet walking
Alone among tombstones
And scares himself so badly

He deteriorates back into
A shepherd carving a crook
In a fairytale as yet written
But lived daily by the worms
That burrow into apples
In search of Eve.

＊ ＊ ＊

The mother—the father—the family—
The overturned car at the bottom of a pond—

Liquor bottles popping to the surface—
Followed by a dunce hat then an
Oil slick where the engine burst—
A policeman retrieves the hat—
The bubbles stop—the pond is quiet
Nothing between our stories now—nothing
Between then and now but
An unrelentingly everywhere—

On the stainless table to
The sound of saws beneath arc
Lights it is decided after trial

And error that the dunce
Hat belonged to the father and is
Now officially a hand-me-down.

* * *

But where is this place—this
Extravagance of fleeting beauty
In the stinkpot of immortality's
Glass privy—is it superstition or
Awakening when—in the amorous
Jaws of a wolf pulling mittens
Out the window of an overturned
Troika—the fingers inside
Uncross themselves—

Innocence can be found in autumn
In the forest around a child waiting
To catch the first falling leaf—.
Who then disappears
Leaving tiny cloven hoof prints
That lead beyond yearning
To the front door of a school.

* * *

Maybe you're neck deep
In a slit trench with a dental pick
Unearthing the fossilized
Remains of Jiminy Cricket

Sometime so far in the future
Robots address you as sir
Or madam in salons where in
Plain view of metal eyes your naked
Leg is shaved with quantum foam.

Why else dig in the dirt for
Remnants of yesterday if not to find
The mirror where it's possible to
See the first time you ran away.

✳ ✳ ✳

When the dead see the living
They shriek—"thar's them ghosts that breathe."

It disturbs their pine box boogie
When we creep inside their sleeping bags—
Bringing moist light—cornfields—seasonal
Accordions—succulents on windowsills—
Coriander and cumin pomades—
Forcing them to feel our sad disturbance
As we shout their names out loud
To no one but ourselves.

✳ ✳ ✳

To say it plainly language may
Describe the most noble thing
Or the encrusted giblets in the coliseum

With equal authenticity—somewhere
A mother awakens underground—

Nursing her first born child—but soon
The earth sends smooth pebbles
And lullabies no one else hears
And for as long as it takes one hand
To crawl out of the dirt to touch

The sun she continues to nurse
That ancient howl into a poem.

* * *

We love how the student
Of the cello begins the piece
In front of the master with a flip
Of lank black hair as if
To ward off circling flies—he lapped
Cream for breakfast which accounts
For the stain on his cummerbund but not
The music in his instrument that
Will not string along with the
Tenuous temerity of topical tenors—

How beside fields of parched corn
At the foreclosed farm sheriffs lean
Against the dead oak while admiring
The nautical skills it took the farmer
To tie the noose around his neck—

The cherry strobe atop the ambulance
Seems to come from the dead man's throat—
Or perhaps it's a new leaf the old
Tree pushes out after past winters
To commemorate every leaf it lost
And now this one—still attached
Until the sheriffs cut it down—

Inside family so much stored
Light—the daughter—the mother—the banker—all
Staring like owls from a dusty loft—
Tangibly home—at the top of the stairs.

* * *

It's sixty years ago—
I'm pinning the corsage on my prom
Date while her parents photograph
The moment before we step
From the stoop into the declining
Years—when this memory fails—
And the photograph fades
And at some seminal level there's
Still blood trickling where I pinned
The flower too close to her breasts—

Her blue eyes were as wide
As a sea between mountains—these revolutions
Around something that comes later

Retain the pink pallor of lips
Freshly kissed for the first time—
These memory we share of that

Apple offered and taken—forbidden to us—
Through the given years we try
But can't remember why.

* * *

The séance goes on—we detach
And attach spirits to anything
Conjured by hope or fear—
The spooky underworld
Peopled by things blood relatives to lint
Inside a pocket watch—

So let's all try somewhere
To reappear—the dead practice every
Second of eternity—they slap
One another on the back hoping
To force a sudden inhale to send
Them tumbling back into a haunting—

We just don't know it
When they do—sitting around
The table holding hands while
Summoning ourselves.

* * *

Regardless of our folly
Believe me the dead are never more
Than one breath away—the smell
Of beeswax mingles with burnt beards
And velveteen settees and suddenly
There are no borders between things
And armed with this knowledge
Ghosts leapfrog candle flames

To escape into the falling rain—
Oh to feel the rain again.

* * *

Changes will come.
The involute of the dissolute
Is the resolute—cages melt—
Wax hardens—flames become
A tongue in the mouth—speaking
A previously unheard poem
That disappears into the truth
No one will hear or say.

A season then—a time spent first
As thought then as speech
Then finally as silence—this—
Then published in diaries
Children read in attics—sneezing

As the dust settles—while parents throw
Expressions at one another
When family affections become
No longer the engine but the caboose
For the entrained touch—

It's the goddess of finite localities
Coring apples with a knife
Honed by worshippers on a throne
Gilded with disbelief where
The consequences of self-absorption
Await like mannikins in windows
That—only when watched—don't move.

✳ ✳ ✳

The man climbing out of the mirror
Is not the only thing to see here
But he holds our attention the way
He holds the spray of violets
Picked from the hill from which
A small stream irrigates
The village where he died—is this
Your father—your brother—
And who else in the mirror
Do you recognize?

Love is beckoning—autumn
Is changing colors inside the dying firefly—

In deep space-while ancestors
Applaud a star is becoming more
Than light—as the tooth spit out on a bib
Is the preface to an epitaph.—

And we in our story—in our personal
Myth stealing fire or pushing
Rocks uphill on some sweaty
Afternoon are scattered or made whole
By the willingness to clean windows
Inside the house of pain.

* * *

In our little valley a glacier
Slid down to become a lake
Where there was a playground
And instead of swings we pushed
Little boats out with each other
Laughing on summer days—

And in the moonlight on those nights when
We stole from our beds to meet beside
The silver water anything seemed possible—
Even saving ourselves from the past.

* * *

Ah—now you remember—the whisper
Of something in your ear—the song

The thrown stone sings falling to earth at peace
With itself where it's found centuries
Later in the same place as pleased
As a boy in overalls with a cowlick
Winning the blue ribbon beside
A pink piglet raised by hand.

The test is to travel then stop—
Over and over again until
There is no difference.

* * *

I know I stayed too long—
Everyone outlives their welcome—
Fish and company stink after three
Days a politician said and who better
To know when things are rotten—

The hand around the glass trembles—
The veins are thick where the skin
Bunches at the wrist—the love in the throat
Is as sweet and young and hot
As peppers dipped in a matador's
Eye—the thing is—moonlight
Excites the empty birches
Simply because nothing is revealed
That doesn't want to be seen—

The mystery is we're here—withstanding
Momentarily the calamitous breathless
Charge before another world begins.

* * *

Out of the rattling shingles overhead
Fruit bats flap toward a bell clanging
As the evening flows into the wire
Connecting it to silence—

Lights come on—a scandal in the barn
Is freeze-framed by halides—a sister
You imagined as an only child struggles
In a poem to unload your father's gun—
Comes to you in the lush tones
Of the bell—one note—pure and clear
Like her—because imagined.

* * *

Nothing is known nor should be
Of the whippoorwill except when it sings.

* * *

There is all at once the rising voices
Above the wind turbine—the fans
Flecked with feathers squealing
On old hinges—powering the ranch—
The dishwasher—the pump causing

The trough to brim with green
Water taken from deep inside the earth

Like a legless creature extracted
From a fable forced to wear shoes.

* * *

Now look—billions—really—
Billions of years have gone by—subways
Are crowded—ghouls make love
To demons to produce zombies—

Mammals experiment with reptiles
In hook-ups in subterranean
Fantasies—pinatas explode on
Commuter trains—not with thunder
But from the spontaneous combustion
Of paperwork so meaningless
It's fatal to read it—

You know this is true—the anthems
Of war are homeopathic extracts
From the hummingbird—

Yet—the couple there—lifting
The weight they can't carry then
Carrying it right up to the edge—
Exhibit the best qualities

Of the shaman who refuses
To answer any questions
But will allow you to borrow the pillow
Where dreams are given bones.

* * *

At the edge of the city—perhaps
The edge of the universe someone is smoking
Da kine and snacking on Pringles—

There's drama in an armchair—
Ashtrays and cushions filled with butts—
Short skirts on the maître-di—
And a robin on the windowsill
So filled with spring light
It merges all realities into a chirp.

* * *

The myth is self-sustaining as long
As one of us distrusts the other
Enough to die for something no one sees
But everyone worships for its
Blushing claw—the chariots
Are stacked and rusting—spears coated
With fluids from a wound—

This is where the echo is stolen
From the whisper then used to rejuvenate

A prophet on his knees spooning illusions
From a broth of baby woodpeckers
Stolen out of a dead tree—unremarkable until
His story kills another tree.

* * *

When uttered from a glandular
Slit foaming with red ribbons images
Of bright light in a barnyard reveal
A tractor a gate and a goat—

We later understand when the child
Is born that this is her home—and the barnyard
Except for the gate is not real—

Though it is the last thing
Anyone will ever see of yesterday.

* * *

Father—each life I chose
I am less and less your flesh—

Mother—each life I make
Is less beholden to your touch—

This is the pendulum attached
To the hand that points to the hour

The time has come to stand up directly
From the root and flower.

This is the arrow in midflight
Believing everything is a target.
Or a receptacle.

This is the arrow returning
Unblooded to the quiver.

This is the uncurling of pure space
At the end of a radiant demise—

We were two young girls—
Or two young boys—
Or a young boy and a young girl—
In a schoolyard beneath spreading
Magnolias catching pink flowers
As they fall then stringing
Them into creature that follow
Us across time and space
Believing we are the trees
They fell out of so long ago.

And we are.

Spell

Spell

She rolls off the couch about three
In the morning—awakened by neighbors or wind
Or the cat on her face or some unholy combination
Of collateral normalcy that trickled from
Her chapped lips—what began as a cram session for finals
Became a party scored by Switchfoot and the trigger
Pop of beer cans and guzzle.

Maybe it was George Jones—maybe it was Vivaldi
Or Mozart or the Stones or Ed Sheerhan or some unknown
With a guitar and a voice like hot honey poured down
A cold hole to a shivering little fairy tale waiting
For warmth to grow its monster wings—each
Generation gives up ground in its own way—

Now the room is empty of songs—botulism
Angels rise from chicken wings near the cold
Stove filling snoring noses on their way
Up the spine to the scarecrow too obsessed
With crows to keep them safe.

She steps on glass on her way to the mirror
To look hard at the ghost looking back at her
As if suddenly the carbon fog on the doorstep
From the truck idling all night in the driveway
With her lover passed out on the wheel
Slipped through a window and dressed

Up just enough to disturb the air with the shape
Of a witch intent on becoming a graduate
Student majoring in mystical glands—

She thinks she's dying—but no—she's only
Speared by morning light—she worries something important
Is missing because she feels a stone break
Windows inside a heart made of glass.

Which is how the night ends when you
Live outside the bebop buried deep
In the biographies others write about you—

She breaks wind on a velvet cushion then smiles
As all of her lovers arise at once from the same
Bed and stagger into the morning
On their way to another mother—she slides slowly
Down the wet staircase where they slept
And enjoys all the years they're gone.

Spell

As the sun sets on the intromittent
Liquid obelisk an orange
Creature spins the rotors on its hat while
Leering down into a reflecting
Pool at its own image.

The photographers documenting
This behavior are amazed to see it engaged
In a ritual mating dance with itself.

The policy hacks changing diapers
On the electorate in an attempt to weaponize
Degrees of verbal flatulence
Blow smoke into the camera lens.

A ubiquitous penis counts the votes
While pharmacies plays Hail to the Thief—

The orange creature rinses the sunrise
From its eyes and successfully
Installs sundown as the new standard
For leadership while the minions
Dig in their ears to recycle the beliefs
That remain fresh as a corpse in the cellar
Of a house where no one lives.

Spell

The stories of the least
Are equal to the stories
Of giants climbing beanstalks
Into sacred nonsense.

On this corner a woman
Is cradling a dog in her arms
That is sustained by the love it receives
While the cardboard around
Them blackens from traffic fumes—
Her mask struggles in the backdraft
Of taxis like shackled words
In the eyes of a mime—

The little dog licks her face.
Suddenly in an updraft a mayfly at the end of its brief
Life lands in a patch of sunlight
Near the woman's hand—its final breath
Erases all suffering.

Seeing this some of us
Refurnish the old story—and some
Hold the dog closer while
Beginning a new one.

Spell

When the alarm goes off
I slide down the shaft in my boots
And fireproof thong prepared
To put on more clothes
Or out fires depending on how
Much smoke is in the air
Around the bent pole.

It's always about descending—
Getting down on the ground
And looking under the furniture
For magnets that found each other.

Looking under every motivation
For the rat that chewed the wires.

Getting back up the pole is the trick—
In between alarms I study the problem—
Practice visualizing an assault
On memories held hostage by the lords
Of abundance dancing with skeletons
Around a burning fuse.

Spell

Maybe I blame a song
Bird slamming into the window
We opened—too late for the bird—to
Keep the smell of broiled lamb
From overwhelming the single
Rose in our daughter's hair—

It's possible to believe
Chopping vegetables into the soup
That shivering inside a flannel robe
Made my hand slip on the knife
And cut so deeply the snapshot
Of a barely remembered lover
Bled out in a trunk in the attic—

But that wouldn't be true—
I need to mention your part in this—
The bowl of soup with gray
Hair floating in clear broth after
Years of two women in love—

The stooped genie in each kiss
Blowing out then relighting candle
After candle in the dark.

Spell

Some doubted Nietzsche's insistence
Language is a bowl from which meaning
Is sipped through a straw—
Others affected to understand
Baudelaire—believing evil is a
Flagpole atop which
Buzzards beshat imperfect eggs—

Facts everywhere. Truth absent.
Except for sunlight on the skaters
Out on the thinnest ice there's
Only this handkerchief dabbing the tears
Of a Mademoiselle afraid of her piano
Whose yellowed ivories ripple
Like flattened tigers in the stinking
Mud beside a waterhole.

At some point I witnessed an event
I'd prefer not to share with anyone
Though I don't mind slicing its flesh
Thin enough to see through—then
Serving it raw on a bedsheet.

That's okay—any more details
Lead to blurting out more than anyone
Wants to know about sage grouse
Tracked by shotguns.

Nietzsche said great wisdom doesn't
Perspire inside dead languages—he thought
Only something like a minnow under
A waterfall might carry ignorance
Upstream to a drooling beard—

He said something about an abyss
But my point—or rather this poem's
Point—is—nothing is looking at you
Except the face of the chauffer
Driving past the point of no return.

We hum like tuning forks attempting
To bring harmony to a sword fight—
We wobble our lips while saying
Prayers that come out in a child's voice
Like wedding vows—origin
Stories turned into fatal strategies
Once astride a throne.

There's no one to help us now—
This is the best news—there's
No one to help us—no one in the air
Is coming down to the ground
To bandage survivors
Or intervene on behalf of the lords
Of myth or gods of retribution for which
The only antidote is disbelief—

It's you and me—in the dark—
Reaching for the light that isn't there
Until we turn each other on.

Spell

The man bending wire around chopsticks
In the name of art inside the offices
Of 21st century institutions famous
For posting wanted posters with generic
Photographs suddenly realizes
He's looking in a mirror at his father—

Now the mobile hangs in space reflecting
The lawn ornaments but not the lawn—
Because—for now—the rough topography
Between being here and there is annihilated by
Instructions for properly wearing a
Pointed hat as well as the relationship
Between suffocation and cutting down
Trees to satisfy a housing boom—

End of the century—beginning of the next—
Day into night—year after year—

So then—how much do children suffer
To walk through the landscapes we
Paint on the air they breathe.

Spell

The brothers kneel beside
The tractor—they're tired—the wrenches
Heavy as sin in the back of the cloak room
Where the priest is fingering . . . beads—
The wheel's flat from an ancient lance point
Run over while breaking the backs
Of spirits in the ground—

The brothers make out smoke
From their shared farm house torn to
Blue bits in the gray sky like herons
Fleeing a tidal wave—

Withdrawal starts with a child seeing
Stars drip from broken bones or
Flour and lard made into bread—wondering
Why this isn't enough to satisfy the
Hunger for the end of time.

There are some things no one
Needs to look at to see—or
To know—that even in a poem—brothers
Can struggle to fix the unfixable—will
Never live long enough to forgive
Or love one another—enough.

Spell

It's a painting of these times—
Rendered without apology for the truth—
Indicating anyone looking too closely
Will be licked by a blood-stained
Tongue—there's a man

And a woman fiddling with napkins
On a lunch break at a table set for three
Beneath the awning of an architecturally
Challenged bistro where the main course
Is served under the table—

Both with a briefcase full of doodah—
They've got tax deductions already planned—
They have ornate wooden tools in velvet
Lined boxes to help lift the nose
In the air when the neck gets tired.

The man smells summer
In the air—stretches in his
Armani cocoon—mentions the fragrance
Of roses to the woman who complains to the waiter
Her steak is not whimpering—

They love one another in the old way—
Or rather—they lift from different trees
During the same storm—flounder in the sky
Long enough to become targets—imagine

A life together with no children—
Then leave without paying the bill.

Spell

In a stable a child is born.
Not for the first time we smell
Donkeys and damp hay and mice
Droppings while wringing birth rags
Beneath a smoking lantern
Held aloft by the doctor whose
Only skill is illuminating midwives
Pulling two worlds apart.

The child's entrance leaves prints
Against the bloody walls of the embassy
Where the mother drags the furniture
With great delicacy out of a mirror
So the guests have places to sit—

We understands the machinery
Drilling into our friends—our planet—
Our child—is dismantled only
By the continuous application of love
To the pieces scattered by fledgling angels who
Throw us out the window while driving
Drunk on imaginary roads—

Maybe it's time to save one another from
The clockwork ghouls who lick
Copper pennies to taste the
Vistas in unseeing eyes—

The dead bump along like shipwrecks
Leaking the antidote for cruelty
Back to the surface to inspire
A prehistoric memory

That worships blood while
Bleeding—that speaks from
All mouths with one tongue the
One word for this shared body
That swims through silence even
As it drowns in chatter—

The one word that when
Spoken unites all beings in love—

The word only you know.

If you can't say it—
Think it.

Spell

The snow brings the neighbors
Swirling with it into the warm
Entry where coats drip from hooks
And dogs run in circles barking
Formal invitations—in the kitchen
Cooks arrange little troughs of pimento
Dip for the bright carrots.

This is a happy place the instant
Before—somewhere—for someone—
The world ends—even here the elderly
Uncle wheezing in a corner chair
With menthol cigarette breath could
Drop off at any moment. Only
The dogs have faith something
Good will fall on the carpet.

There's a knock at the door—
It opens inward like all revelation—

The giant snowman from the front
Yard made by neighborhood kids
Walks in with a carrot nose
And briquettes eyes—we're
Of course stunned by any evidence
Of magic—though it's everywhere—
Without asking, the snowman
Carries off carrot sticks from every
Plate back into the winter.

"I guess that gentleman wants to assure
He'll always have a nose," says the Uncle
Through a spume of blue smoke—stubbing
A Kool in the dessert and clearly
The only one to believe this happened.

Believing everything you see
And everything you don't see
At the same time is the death
Of pre-conception—the beginning
Of independence—of slow romances—

Of falling in love with the new faces
Visible through the glorious keyhole
Where the secret copulations between
The ordinary and the sublime

Advances the next fiction
Someone will die to defend.

Spell

The years go by—nothing changes
Except the ashtray on the mantle fills
With nose rings left from a party held
So long ago the girls who wore them
Are now in the kitchen drinking sloe gin
In tea cups while combing one another's silver hair—
Remarking how liberating
It once felt to blow smoke at a man—

No one smokes anymore—
But the ashtray can't go back to its
Life as a home for hermit crabs—
The interior is no longer luminous pearl
With highlights of violet—just dark from
Stubs though still nacreous with eel.

All the women went away—except
The one who's still here—alone—
With her memories—underwater—
The girl locked in the woman—the woman
Inside the exalted shell the tide takes
Out and brings back in—the waves a spilled mirror
Reflecting the fiction and the grace of
Those shipwrecked years.

Spell

Nana took the screen
Door off the hinges to scrub
Away the fly specks—

She rolled her hose down to both
Knees and her blouse up to the elbows—then
Pulled wire brushes from the suds
While crooning a Ruth Etting song.

With the screen door removed the
Neighbors could see the children
Peeking from the shadows in the house
As if they lived in a prologue inflicted
On them by laboratory mice—

We trusted no one back then—
But worshipped the goddess who
Kept our only exit clean.

Spell

The veterans of the diplomatic
Wars fold their berets in the appropriate
Revolutionary Guard manner made popular
In Foreign Legion movies—they twist
Purple-knobbed fingers around long sticks
That slide miniature tanks and battleships
Across polished tables like croupiers
Pushing chips at losers.

Somewhere a soldier is staring
Through a scope through blowing sand
At an object staring back at her—one of
Them will fire first and the momentary
Addition of color will be no more significant
Than the bloody nose of an oxygen
Starved climber planting a flag
On a snow-covered height.

Who will comfort these last things—
Who will call the red puddle mother—
Whose tears will irrigate the harvest—what
Shadow will grow bones in midair—when
Will the aggregate light of the crowd be brighter than
The twinkle in the hangman's eye.

Spell

Under the directions of a skilled hypnotist
The Count—that bedeviled little man
With forked beard and rabbit eyes—recalls forbearers
Dressed in pelts—smelling of cave seep—
Poking white grubs from logs with sticks
Then eating them alive—swallowing
Rodents—dancing around the fire
Inside lightning-struck trees—

These newly discovered family secrets
Are humbling enough to put an end for two days to
Berating servants for leaving dust
On the bust of his father—who fell from
His horse while retreating at the Battle of Lützen—
Who passed on his entire estate
And swinish manners to his son.

Now the Count is under the hypnotic spell
Of an equally unscrupulous man—he is made
To walk around the office like a chicken—puck—puckha—
Told to hatch a burgundy pillow—to peck
The white thread in the Persian carpet—

When he awakens he goes home—
And polishes his father's bust.

Spell

The little boy pulls the covers
Up under his chin and listens
To his brother making soft noises
In the bottom bunk as the wind
Moves the curtains around the open
Window just enough to see
The branches of the lindens
Fingering holes in the storm.

It's hard to sleep on nights like this—
When the world is between familiars
Or as the little boy thinks of it
When the creek turns into a river
And the stepping stones
Are the bald heads of grandfathers
Holding their breath underwater
For children to walk across.

Little brother gently snores.
The curtains grow still.
The morning light erases the stars.
It's time to wake up.

And against all odds
Some of us do.

Spell

The smoke drifts out of the ground
From an unmarked grave in a forest
Near Verdun—a slight depression between trees
With mushrooms ringed in the shape
Of a narrow green ellipse.

It's easy to say smoke because there's
No word, even in French, for what lives in the air
As substance that can't be seen—

Cowslip blooms white
In the silence before dawn.
Beauty is trabecular to function
But in tomorrow's light the skein
Of lilies clenched atop a rotted uniform
Seems a betrayal of all lost causes.

The dead come back to the ones
They died to protect—not as a face
In an elevator or a shawl wrapped around
A rescue dog but as nightlight haloing
A cradle or the first tentative uncurling
Flag lifting from the blackened
Soil after wildfire notifying the sun
What's green will rise again

Spell

Magic is everywhere but one must
Walk barefoot through it—
Curse it like mud and hail and burrs
Until—exhausted—the disbeliever
Surrenders to the black-robed birds
Pecking distance from the eyes
Of frozen mountaineers—

There's always a stoop with children
Playing hopscotch on pavement
Smudged by charcoal rings where last
Independence Day firecrackers went off or maybe
The apple in the lunchbox exploded—

They braid grass into keepsakes
To celebrate a time when the sound of bees
And smell of clover were a minuete
Circling slow wagons around innocence
At the end of a saw-toothed road leading
To a pond where thoughts wait
For a tongue to fish them out—

The smoke from the fetish—which—let's face
It—has something to do with a loin cloth
Too loose and too porous to be a thong—
Settles around a citizen's face to quiet the bee
Inside long enough to steal its mon—er—honey—

We could talk about the fog from the white
Powder in the blackened spoon obscuring
The lecherous clown unmasked behind
A dumpster while besmirching the rag he swore
To protect—but that only explains
How the fuse got lit—

Which—briefly—makes a hero out of
The baby who—using the only weapon
It has—shoots a projectile through
An open window to score a direct hit
On a diaper hanging from a pole—

The warming is complete—the devastation
Of deodorants and roach paste finally pinned
The tail on the ecological donkey—there are still
Rivers—they're red as the headwaters
Of an open wound—unable to carry
The reflections of trees or sky—only
The buoyant remnants of the bottom line—

Nothing remains but a single ice cube
In the claw of a hot machine and the
Music like candle wax under fingernails—
Emitting weird implications—creaking
Organ soloes—painting the choir
With the bad breath of connoisseurs
That bottle and sell the ricochet—

Let's admit it—we are the children
Braiding grass on that forgotten stoop—

Smelling the burnt coconut smell
Of the fuse inside the lunchbox becoming a dark stain
On the frock worn by an elderly priest
Walking a small rat right up to the porch—
Over and over—leaflets galore—
As if trapped in a shaken
Bottle of landscapes with no sky—

Time to take everything off—even
The skin—to put it all back
On—to proximate what is real
And what is good into a distinction
Not unlike an astronomer cleaning
Her eye instead of her lens . . .

Our song starts in deep inkling—
The ambedo of the spirit dance—the
Candle lit in another room—the world
In headlong assault on newly
Formed senses—from the first
Cry in the cradle—until the last croak
Along a stream as stars fall—the hypnotic
World streaming into every cell—
Grateful for us—its receivers—

Shining from every river—
Face and flower and in underground cities
Beneath the lilies where the red light
Is always on—the candle brightens
The edges of the jumping off place
Beyond which forgiveness waits
Downstream and upstream
Of goodbye.

Spell

Grandma was a witch they said
In the farmhouses around
Her chunk of hilly ground where
She eked out a living midwifing
And selling herbs and eggs
And sometimes quilts
Once the city slickers discovered
Her patterns at a county fair.

There were the beheadings.
Once the chickens stopped laying eggs
They were killed then smoked or
Canned for winter meals.

She'd slide into the henhouse
And come out with a chicken by
Both legs hanging down from her left
Hand with a cleaver in the right
And in a single motion flip
The chicken up while cutting off
It's head in mid-air with the other
Hand—she was good at
It and I never saw her miss.

But oh my those dead chickens—
Fluttering around the yard with no
Head until something upstairs
Communicated to something downstairs
That the end was old news.

I hope I don't do that.
Pick up from my death bed
And flop around the house
Although if that happens I'd like to—
Even briefly—scare the ones
Watching into understanding

There's plenty of work left to do—
Happen—while you can.

Spell

Maude lifts the powder puff
To gently shake out the lilac
Scented talcum before tapping
Her armpits. Even though she
Shaved them a week ago when
She bathed they're still
Fresh as trout in a creel.

Look says one diner—a vision—
Where—say the guests looking in all
Directions except the one where Maude
Grips the banister—flowering in
The vase of her décolletage.

There's little doubt everyone
Saw something but only William
Saw her throat redden in anticipation
Of carving the roast.

If I were there—if I were a man
Instead of a spirt living outside
His time—I would have held
Her chair—whispered the language
Of roses instead of gargling the shabby
Beaujolais with the fleshpots.
Maude would have seen me—
Not through me—I would
Stop her glance and the whiteness

Of her smile would shine forever
In my grave like a biblical star.

Indeed—one of the guests—
Feeling my presence—reached
Under the table and squeezed
What he thought was her thigh
But was only my tangible regard.

What a night for poetry.
Beauty above—and under—the table—
The balustrade emptied
Momentarily of velvet goblins
In turned up shoes—verses bursting
In every mouth after the flesh
Is swallowed—*mon Dieu*—this poetry

Of refinement—of satiation—these liquid
Hosannas and other partitas of rut.

Spell

Walk into the desert where your fate
Drinks hidden pools of rain beneath
Skies mild with circling doves.

It's enough perhaps to wake up
In the ambulance with the siren coming
From the driver's mouth as medics kiss
You so deeply you feel a tongue
Desecrating the beautiful sunrise
Where possible new poems smolder.

There's no heart left for the fight—

But the heart never was in it—it's
The mind that wants a punching bag—the mind
That severs the rope just before
Reaching the top—it's the bloody *venatores*
Dragging a speared lion toward

The president in the front row—
These beneficiaries of excess sipping
Melted gold from leather cups while
Placing bets on the outcome
Of a preordained disgrace.

Spell

The appearance of the moral police
Initiates shrieks from picnickers
On the banks of an industrial canal—
They confess to the sin of hoping
We aren't the last thing they see—

The blue heron with the two-headed
Fish nods up—and down—up—and
Down—she's just an oil derrick above a dry well
Pumping the will power of citizens
From the agonized ground.

Everyone has a license to smile
In their allotted years—
Overwhelmed by the courage
Of flowers pushing through
A crust of snow—these blue
Faces alive when winter clamps
Forceps on the stem—we whisper to
Love and shout at shadows.

Soldiers will die for cause or comrade—
But only poets will die for a rose.

Spell

There's a lichened white wall
Struggling to stay up
After the rest of the church
Collapsed from the weight
Of bat shit and whispered prayers
Undermining the foundation
Like infection in a wisdom tooth.

The wall provides shade for families
To dry their sweaty bandanas
On the shattered bottles that line
The top like razors in a candy bowl—
Many carved their names in the cracked
Adobe to indicate they exist and to honor
A soulful look through the window
Of dreams where a lonely figure
Brings bandages from the other side . . .

Tonight when there's no moon
They will take one another's hand
Before crossing that arbitrary border between different
Ways to arrange cut flowers.

Spell

In a headscarf made of second-
Hand long-johns died brown
To hide the stains—my Auntie
Wanders through the sweet gum
And sugar maples as late autumn
Rain drips from the orange leaves.

She carries roots in her apron—
Drinks the bitter water from
The elbow of a crooked pine—

Memories live beneath the scarf
Golden and beautiful and lost
As last year's vital signs.

Auntie worked all her life to ignore
The dripping beards of the men
Entering through the kitchen door
With feathers stuck to the blood
On their boots—she succeeded only
As long as it took winter
To cover their graves with snow.

(Except the ghost beneath
The snow looking up at the fox
About to step in the trap—it signals
The fox but it's too late—too
Many winters between the living

And the dead for understanding that
Each belongs to each and only
The purple lupines in the brothel
Of a summer field accept this enough
To let go the bee in their bloom.

In memory everything fades—
The snow is white—the ghosts
Are white and no one can really
Presume to say why ravens relocated parts
Of the bride to this battlefield)

Now that the leaves are gone
And the forest is bare I
Am the one left to keep Auntie
From dissolving into the little
Creek that flows out of the photo albums where
The lessons taught to children
To honor and obey the silence between
Trees or parents turns to gunfire
Beneath a whirling weather vane.

Spring will arrive—
Blood will sing to blood across
Immeasurable distances in octaves
Beautiful and unbearable to hear—

My auntie climbs over the fence
With a song in her pocket—the sun drops
Down in a purple hush—childhood
Ends when the light begins to change.

Spell

If we're lucky there's a sacred place
Inside our memories we enter
With no more effort than lying
In the grass on a warm day with clouds
Drifting through blue rooms
Without walls behind our eyes—

A temple devoid of faith or collateral
Or psalms or worship filled with the
Ones we loved but couldn't save.

I'm there now—with you—
Our eyes open—seeing everything
Then and nothing now but the clouds

And the scary figures through
The dirty window that are benevolent
Once we clean the glass—see—the two
Doves flying out of our bodies
With strands of our hair to build
A nest in the last tree standing.

Spell

The morning the gunfire stopped
I heard the sound of a small girl playing.
Her voice stood out against the silence—
A winter leaf refusing to fall
Despite the killing cold.

Meanwhile everything inside
Went numb—a blank wall no graffiti
Artists would tag for fear the wall
Might write back on them.

I'm the message for the world
Left inside an empty gun—

I'm saying not a single photon
Shines on the next moment
Until we personally light it up—

I'm saying the ghost of a small
Girl playing is what's left to love until
The ammunition runs out.

Spell

★ ★ ★

Doctors bear the weight of illness
Like oxen yoked to a cart they can't pull—

We hear other sounds—waves on
Reefs lifting plankton toward the moon.
Dream of people in little villages
Beside muddy water saying goodbye
In another language—hissing like Rilke's
Hand on fire when he pushed
It through the frozen page.

★ ★ ★

A falcon climbs from the steam—
A doctor of disorder and shadow
In orbit above figures digging
A hole for themselves—the falcon
Waits for whatever escapes
The inquisition of shovels
To supply a remedy for birth.

★ ★ ★

Imagine you write all night—
Or speak every day about the grass
Growing on a southern slope—a derrick drifting
On greasy waves—a thin snake
Circling in the mangroves—imagine
The lonely thought without a mind—

And when it seems impossible
To believe in someone or anything anymore
The falcon lands on the empty page
And the next moment begins.

Spell

The prince was never the same
After getting lost for three days
Among the murmurings of the forest.
He followed ripe blueberries deeper
Into thickets near the castle—hearing
The servants call his name—

Shivering in torn purple—the wild boars
Snorting somewhere on his trail—
His highness broken near a shining
Stream lying still as a lapis
Eye in an amber petroglyph.

The hot sunlight warmed his
Splintered anklebone.

I watched this—yes I was
In the trees with a worm when
The prince fell from his nest.

He was found crushing
Bluebonnets under his nose
To remind him of his pillow
And his mother's hair.

He grew old and quiet.
He never talked about the owls.
He only once said—who—

When asked what angels do
When no one's left to save.

Spell

Sunlight dapples the aromatic herbs—
We find the pestle where it fell last Summer
Among the rosemary—crush
The lavender flowers until there's room
To crush more—don't forget—
Remember—Joan of Arc was sold
By the English but burned in France saying—
"I am not afraid—I was born to do this"

The winter is an ocean around
The unwritten page—bound with
Neglect or reverence—this book of shadows—
Brief with creatures—some snared
In stories—others evaporating in mouths
Alongside recycled promises—

This fire consumes everything
But first it brightens the library
Of those who came and those to come
Where we enter a silver corridor—shelves
Lined with tales of acquisition—each authored—
Signed—and titled—*not mine.*

Liquid Spell

Day 1

who will ask that child to be quiet?
not me though her crying
betrays us to the soldiers patrolling
the edges of hope where children
seldom stop crying even when
held to hush them.

as we walk we make up stories
in hopes the stories will outlive us.
as we walk we remember the war.
as we walk we remember the swish
of machetes taking our cattle.

as we walk we remember the grandmothers.
as we walk we remember the taste
of precious milk from the goat.
as we walk we tend the wounds
of the elders and the last goat.

many don't get this far.

over the next dune the sea
waits within a cracked bowl of blue—
source of tears—the salt water
inside the dream.

many don't get this far.

all through the days and nights
with the desert stars watching we
leave a trail the soldiers follow—

but the sea calls—a blue beckon—
and if the soldiers are slow or we are silent
and worship the right gods at the right time
the soldiers will find only the things we
couldn't carry and see an ancient ship
beyond the range of their rifles.

you might ask what we who
have so little couldn't carry—

and I look at the black-haired
little girl in my arms and the bones of
black-eyed boy their father holds
and know there is nothing else—
everything else is yesterday's light
which is too heavy to carry.
Many don't get this far.

Day 2

we load into the decrepit
boat as the waterline creeps up
the sides so it is possible
to trail a hand in the blue
that is all that's left of everywhere—

the sky and water are details
keeping apparitions from entering
a maze of hues with no clues
to why they came or where they is.
trawler the smuggler says
loading us carefully so there is equal
weight on both sides to keep from
capsizing if the wind picks up—

some families are split apart—
like ours—by weight—we stare across gunnel
to gunnel at one another—

father stare across at child—mother stare
across at father—daughter at brother—

goat bones bleaching in the dunes
where militia ate her.

she was what we could not carry.

Day 3

already a grandfather
went overboard in the night.

he just let go after holding
on—he just let go—
many of us heard the splash
but in the dark mistook
it for waves slapping the boat
as if birthing it.

the grandfather leaned into me
for three days rocking inches
above the waterline murmuring a quiet
song I didn't know—humming
without moving his lips—maybe
a prayer I think now—maybe
a curse I think now—
in the morning he is gone.

now the singing turns
to a groaning song way back
in the throat as if a ghost is loosed
where the heartbeat ends—

by now the food is gone
and the wind picks up and sharks
follow the boat and if they were
friendly I could touch one—

pet one with my hand but they
watch with the grandfather in their smile.

Day 4

we are told the journey
to the safe place takes 7 days
and the boat we are on is
a 10 day boat so we should feel
lucky to have 3 extra days
to find our home before the boat
sinks under us—even so says

this smiling jinn—you might have
to swim the extra mile.

so it is only hope—still following
like a goat set free but lonely
for companionship—that steers us
through the waves—hope—
that if it were a meal—would feed
everyone but only once.

Day 5

when I look across I see
immediately no eyes meet mine
in the temple of the loving gaze where
my husband and I share this
journey from our separate sides
of the sinking boat—

in the heat the boat smells
of old fish—the guts of the fish
only the fish knows—the
fish dreaming of ice cream—

no—that's not right—I am
thinking of sherbets and ice creams
and melons and honey on a spoon—
the fish in this boat are
like that husband—no—my husband—
gone into the sea—into
a sort of writing made by waves
and wind that even in
my dazzled state of blue seems
to explain why hope burns
itself so we can see it.

Day 6

i wander inside the temple
of the loving gaze with my husband
even though he's gone—my daughter
believes he guides us underwater
but I know better because he
can't swim though he is a beautiful
man on the earth so I don't
correct her but agree
her daddy watches over us.

it is disconcerting but not really
to see we are starting to sink
and only a few of the women
have the strength to throw the water
back to the water with cupped hands.
the stars are out and I see
the dead I will be reaching toward
the ghost inside of me and just

then my son goes overboard
and the thrashing of sharks in the dark
somehow stimulates the sun to
turn into a red morning.

Day 7

it is the sound that prods
us awake but once awakened I see
my daughter is beside me—pointing
while trying to speak through
lips crusted over with prayers
that died unspoken and words she
hasn't learned and words
i hope she never will.

she points at the sound—

she points at the white gulls
unexpectedly silent hovering
with glittering malice in the
old stone old gray coastal air.

she points to the waves
piling up in white foam—she
points to where blue ends
and other colors begin.
she is pointing at the fig trees
filled with ripe fruit and coconuts
falling beneath gently swaying
palms—the soft thud—so unlike a rifle butt
against a door—the sound heard above
the wave's lengthy hiss—

she points at the nurses
beside tents with red crosses
and she is pointing at hope
in full glory throwing scarves
of red silk so high they take years
to flutter down and she is pointing
to the shade of a peacock tree—

beneath which my husband
and my son are unpacking their faces
so we are back in the temple

of the loving gaze—between fatal shores—
in the one home we never leave.

Spell

Spell

Then the small animals got to speak
And with one voice they requested the giant
Sequoias to intervene on their behalf
By covering the world with a botanical spray of hope
Driven up the heartwood toward the sky
From the consciousness of Earth—

The large animals agreed—the lame
Creatures agreed—the wildflowers asked
Questions but eventually came around
While the humans groused and grunted
And turned various shades of colors
That bled into one color used
To decorate the inside of the hole where
The groundhog counts the days.

Finally it was settled—no one will
Ever again walk through the door of another's
Flesh without first knocking and receiving
Permission and even then they must
Leave behind as offering an opening
That won't close but never bleeds.

Spell

Most don't know what others
Mean by love—only what they
Learned from time spent riding
The hour hand around the clock—

One feels it by kissing the reflection
In the still waters of the heart—

One knows it in the smell
Of wet fur dreaming by a fire—
One beside a grave listening
To the sermon before throwing
Dirt on a child—one will
See it in a glass of wine—one
In a bowl of good smoke—or alone
In wilderness when mice crawl
Into our boots to lick the salt—

I see it in the footprints
Drying on the wood floor where
She walked barefoot from the bath
Then flew out to the moon through
Window glass that didn't break.

Spell

The habaneros burn for hours after
Chopping them into the posales unless
You wash your hands—even then—
They swell bee-stung and hot
As the memory of vinyl seats
In the convertible out front
Of the church where you sang
In a voice yet cracked about old
Wooden crosses besides girls
You hoped might dance with you—

Years later the car seats
Are still hot—even as the snow
Covers the fields and there's nothing
But the sweep of it falling
And the song in the wooden cross
Burns on the wind every time
You unzip these memories
And fall asleep on the horn.

Spell

It was during a heat wave
Somewhere near the equator
With blue and orange birds almost
Speaking Spanish on the strangely
Gray branches of the limp banyans
When the map lost its borders
And became as simple as a frozen pond
Beneath descending geese—

In the course of opening the door
On the way out a shiver ran up my spine—turned
Into a cramp that became a spasm
That ended as a seizure that threw
Me across the space/time continuum
Out to the far flung reaches of the stars
While my body—that old saddle—
Lay on the floor impervious
To the falling rain.

I don't mind rubbing oil on the saddle
Knowing when I return from those heights
It won't creak under my weight—
And even my enemies won't
Know I'm coming.

Spell

The roof blows off—we wish
On missiles like falling stars—dust billows
In from the west—where all dust begins—
So thick we can't see what we're drinking
But it tastes faintly like looking away—
Of copper discs on the eyes of friends
Licked so they'll stay in place.

Another bomb close enough
To kick the juke box on and someone
Dances alone through the dust—we don't know
Anything for sure anymore other than this
Is the Electric Prunes singing
I Had Too Much To Dream Last Night.

We see the glowing red mountains
Of ash and the swollen brown reeds
Around a dry canal where a
Wingless bird hops on one leg—its
Face is a spring tide in which
We ebb into one another
Then flee back into solitude.

Is this why we were born—
To light each other up then blow
Smoke across the void
Like beekeepers stunning

A hive before stealing
Something precious—the taste
Of another in our mouths—

The honey poured over blood
Becoming words even the gods
Know enough not to say—

But we say them—
And something dies
When we do.

Spell

To do something simple—
Make bread from grain planted
By seed—thinned when it's lush—
Stooped under a bandana all
Summer into Fall—the wheat
Blessed by weather—ripened
By distant fire—something simple—like
Turning water and clay on a wheel—
The bowl teaching you all there is
To know about empty and full.

Love might be so tender
And brave it stays in the sinking heart
As the lifeboats row away.

Something simple—like right now—
The strategic placement of lips
To an anthill—whispering into
The small opening—I love you—Earth—
Air—Water—Fire—Ant.

Love and Gratitude To My Parents
And Teachers—Visible As Well As Invisible—

In Particular

Jenny Van West
Hanno Giulini
Anne Jablonski
Norman Dubie
Carie Garret
Clint Willis
Sharon Doubiago
Michael & Jamie Foster
Alicia Mathias
Erich Schiffmann
John Huey
Nick Hill
Xulia Duran-Rodriquez
Dirk Nelson
Kelly Lee
Alexis Rhone-Fancher
Sam Hamill

I am also deeply grateful to Red Hen Press and their amazing staff for the support and trust I've received over the years. Especially the invaluable counsel and contributions made to this book by Kate Gale, Mark Cull, Tobi Harper Petrie, Monica Fernandez and Rebeccah Sanhueza—you have my heart.

BIOGRAPHICAL NOTE

Gary Lemons has written poetry since 1965. He attended Bread Loaf Writers' Conference in 1971 and 1972 and graduated from the Undergraduate Poetry Workshop at the University of Iowa in 1975. He has studied with some of the great poets of his and any generation, including Norman Dubie, Maxine Kumin, William Stafford, John Berryman, Diane Wakoski, and Donald Justice, none of whom are to blame for what he made of their guidance. He has published eight books of poetry, including *The Snake Quartet*. Of the many things he's done to support his writing, he's most grateful for the time spent reforesting clear-cuts in the PNW where he planted over 500,000 trees. He lives in Port Townsend, Washington, between the sea and the mountains, with his life partner Nöle Giulini, to whom this and all his books are dedicated.